12/29/98

A B C D

E F G H

I J K L

M N O P

Q R S T U

V W X Y

Z

Nedobeck's Alphabet Book

by

Don Nedobeck

P.O. Box 20737   Milwaukee, WI 53220

ISBN 0-944314-00-7

Alvin
Alligator sits in
An
Armchair eating
An
Apple.

B

Bosco
Bear
Bathes in his
Bathtub with a
Blue
Brush and a
Boat.

C

Cathy
Cat and her pet
Canary
Care for her
Cactus.

D

Darryl
Duck
Dives
Daringly.

Edna
Eagle sits on her
Eggs in her nest in an
Elm tree.

F

**Freddie
Frog gives
Flowers to his
Friend
Florence.**

G

Gale
Gabs with
Gordon, her
Great
Gray
Goose.

H

Henrietta
Hen
Has a
Horrendous
Hairdo.

I Ivan eats an
Ice-cream cone
In the winter on his
Igloo.

J

Jeremiah
Jackrabbit wears his
Jade green
Jacket and eats a
Jam sandwich.

M

**Merrill, the
Maroon
Monkey,**

N

Nibbles
Nine
Nutritious
Nuts
Neatly.

O

Oscar, an
Ornery
Old
Owl,
Oversees his
Orange grove.

P

Pudgy
Paul
Pig
Plows through his
Pail of
Pears.

Q

Queen
Quintessa's
Quaint
Quail
Quartet croons
Quietly while
Quentin listens.

R

Reggie, the
Redwing blackbird,
Races his plane
Right through the
Rain.

S Sidney
Sparrow
Soars through a
Sunlit
Sky.

T

Terri,
The
Tall,
Thin
Tan
Tiger,
Talks with
Three
Tiny
Toads by
Their
Toy
Truck.

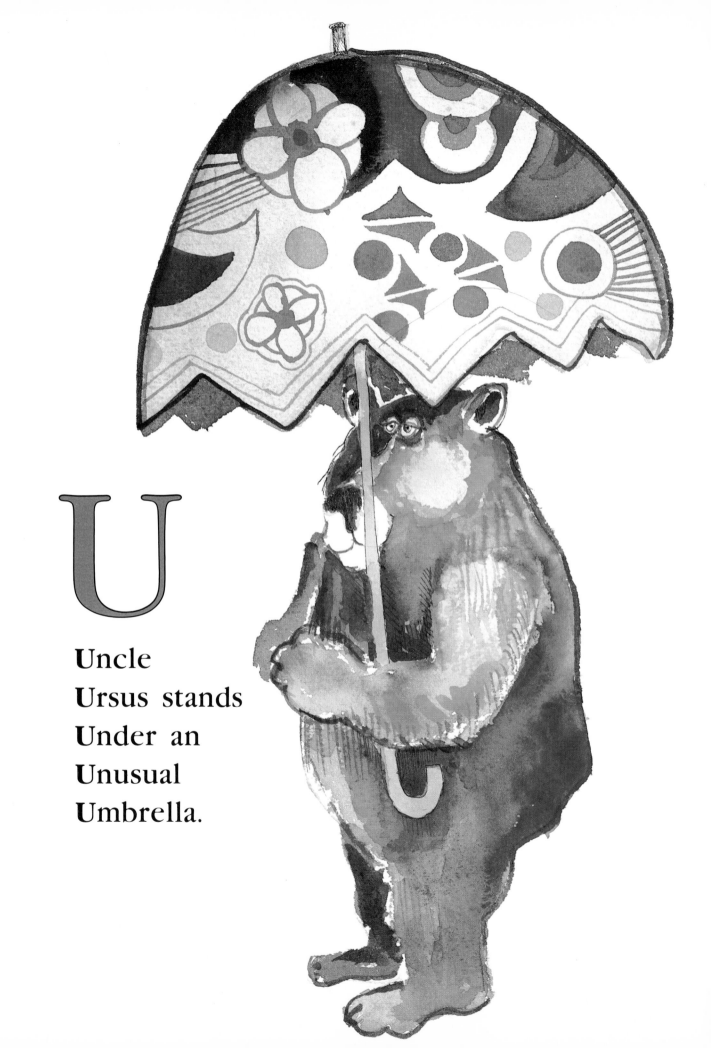

U

**Uncle
Ursus stands
Under an
Unusual
Umbrella.**

Vincent plays his **V**iolin for **V**ictoria in a field of **V**iolets.

W

Wanda
Witch
Whisks through the
Windy night on her broom
With her
White cat,
Walter.

Xavier plays his **X**ylophone.

Y

Yvonne, the
Yellow
Yak,
Yawns.

Zola
Zebra snores with
Zig-
Zagging
Z's.

A B C D

E F G H

I J K L

M N O P

Q R S T U

V W X Y

Z